T0195862

Nature Whispers

AS THE

Trees Speak

CHRISTINE J.K. KANAKIS

BALBOA.PRESS

A DIVISION OF HAY HOUSE

Balboa Press books may be ordered through booksellers or by contacting:

Balboa Press
A Division of Hay House
1663 Liberty Drive
Bloomington, IN 47403
www.balboapress.com
844-682-1282

Because of the dynamic nature of the Internet, any web addresses or links contained in this book may have changed since publication and may no longer be valid. The views expressed in this work are solely those of the author and do not necessarily reflect the views of the publisher, and the publisher hereby disclaims any responsibility for them.

The author of this book does not dispense medical advice or prescribe the use of any technique as a form of treatment for physical, emotional, or medical problems without the advice of a physician, either directly or indirectly. The intent of the author is only to offer information of a general nature to help you in your quest for emotional and spiritual well-being. In the event you use any of the information in this book for yourself, which is your constitutional right, the author and the publisher assume no responsibility for your actions.

Any people depicted in stock imagery provided by Getty Images are models, and such images are being used for illustrative purposes only. Certain stock imagery © Getty Images.

Print information available on the last page.

ISBN: 979-8-7652-3103-6 (sc)
ISBN: 979-8-7652-3101-2 (hc)
ISBN: 979-8-7652-3102-9 (e)

Library of Congress Control Number: 2022912715

Balboa Press rev. date: 07/22/2022

To my grandmother, Lela Traver,
who asked me to document my communications
with Nature and Spirit

Contents

Thousands of books upon the shelves,
each a testimony to
someone pursuing a true self...

Preface

I suppose the purpose of all writing is to understand oneself more completely. What else could it be? When I walk into a bookstore and spot an interesting title, I glance around and see thousands of other volumes of the written word, waiting silently for someone to notice them.

What causes me to be attracted to this particular book? Ultimately, it is the need to find out more than I am already conscious of, or perhaps it is to connect with a person or spirit who is on a parallel path of self-discovery.

My grandmother once suggested that I write a bit each day. I tried several years ago and threw out most of what I wrote about my spiritual experiences because I had the fear that someone would find them, read them, and mock me. I no longer have that fear. My experiences in life have taught me that fear only stagnates growth and postpones understanding the truth within myself.

Each day is unique. What is it I experienced today that helped me to know "me" better? Each new dawn provides an opportunity to scrap old patterns of thinking that block progress and pushes me into an adventure of self-discovery.

May I cleanse my own mind and heart and house and not worry about someone else's.

Clearing Clutter

As I sit here in my office and gaze around the space, I notice that every corner is filled with cabinets and boxes stuffed with "invaluable" things long forgotten. I never used to collect things. I am not sure why this accumulation has manifested. There must be a little message in this having happened. I must be very careful about what objects I keep. They seem to multiply exponentially before my eyes! Certainly they have an energy all their own that affects all around.

Do I really need this? Is that something I can give away? I wonder how useless these poor items must feel sitting on shelves for years and years, not being noticed, admired, or used.

At another level, the thoughts that accumulate in my mind must have an energy all their own that affects all around. Which ones do I want to keep? Which ones do I want to delete?

Metaphor for My Mind

Clear the clutter from my mind;
Thoughts upon thoughts
Leave me blind.

Clear the clutter,
Poison ivy of the mind.
Clip entangled vines that bind.

Pruned away now,
Useless past behind,
Thoughts depart, leaving
Peace of mind.

Coincidence? Serendipity?
Manifestations of the Mind?

Yesterday I was sitting with a student at her dining room table when my eye caught notice of a bouquet of magnificent blue hydrangeas. They were as large as pom-poms! They adorned the table's center and were a delight to see. I secretly thought how wonderful it would be to have a bouquet like these.

This morning I showered, dressed, and walked out the door to find the gardener and his son striding toward me with a beautiful bouquet of the same type of flowers I saw yesterday—blue, with a mix of purple. I was wonderstruck to notice that God heard my little prayer and inspired this family to present these flowers to me on my day of birth. What a perfect day it is to receive a marvelous surprise and to notice how we can all be divine instruments without being aware of it, just as were the gardener and his son.

Connections with All Elementals: Biodynamic Farming

While enrolled in a yearlong biodynamic farming course at Chestnut Ridge, New York, I experienced life-changing impacts that led to my expanded understanding of the unity of all creation. At no other time in my life while undergoing formal education was I so inspired as with my biodynamic farming immersion. We students were taught how each part of our universe affects the well-being of all here on earth, and also how all that we do on earth affects the well-being of the universe.

The notes I took were written in poetic form. The spontaneity of these writings shocked me. This is my testimony to the miracle of experiential education.

Instinct-Intuition

Instinct-Intuition,
What happened to you?
Where have you gone?

Hidden by life's distractions,
Impatience,
Greed,
Take heed.

Lost connections—disconnections
Result in not knowing when to plant,
Where to plant,
How to plant.
Oh my!

Instinct-Intuition,
Where have you gone?
O Cosmos, please help us reconnect
So we may once again beget
True living,
Oneness with all.

Instinct-Intuition,
Please give me a call!

Inner Planets, Outer Planets

May the rhythms of the inner planets
Pulsate through my life:
Moon,
Mercury,
Venus.

Short cycles, annual plants, and tides;
The lime connection drawing water to itself,
Sublime;
Earth's formative forces—
All these connect with human desire, reproduction, emotion, and
the heart.

Outer planets help us too:
Mars,
Jupiter,
Saturn.

Longer cycles happen now with
Easygoing
Flowing perennials.

Cosmic forces here apply,
Very laid back,
No need to attract.

Highly content is Silica:
Cosmic in nature,
It has found its resting place,
Undemanding and homeopathic in stature.

Stepbrother Clay enters here,
Gravitating between Silica (outer perception)
And Lime (outer desire).
Silica is Clay's favorite,
His most dear.

Carbon, Oxygen, Hydrogen, Sulfur

Four siblings are we
To brother Nitrogen, who mediates us
Ever so patiently,
Skillfully.

Nitrogen assumes in Carbon,
And with the help of Sulfur
A new spirituality is formed
That is Astrality!

Now Nitrogen drags brother Oxygen
So he can link with Carbon.
The new couple escapes in a new form—
Carbon dioxide!

Nitrogen and Oxygen may seem dead
When in the air,
But watch out!
As they enter the soil,
They are such an active pair—
Alive, so alive,
Like bees in a hive.

Hydrogen dissolves and disperses everything.
He creates Chaos.
He carries out into the universe and brings back in.
Chaos in seed meets Chaos in periphery.
Look out!
New life comes about.

The Whole

A healthy mix,
Just the right blend
Of earth, water, air, heat,
Plants, insects, animals, and minerals:
Elements—elemental spirits too!

All give,
All take.
Together all create
The whole.

Planets and stars look down on our farms.
They spew blessings from the heavens,
Forces infused with all that Nature uses.

Large, small,
Size matters not at all.
For in the end each makes the perfect blend
Of what is needed to continue
This cycle of life that
We humans are a part of.

Pruning

We climbed her limbs with saws in hand
And chose a branch to prune.
Should it be this one?
Should it be that?
In the end, thank God, it matters not!

I chose the branch—
Or did the branch choose me?
I began to saw as hard as can be.
The teeth got stuck in that "honored" branch—
Oh no!
Not a simple task.
Tried again and again.
Stuck once more.

I glanced up and said,
"Let me try one last time."
Took a deep breath and let the saw glide gently
To and fro, to and fro,
So easily did the branch of the tree let go.

A grand lesson was learned that day:
The results of my actions will be bright
If I saw lightly, live lightly,
With much to gain without much pain
To the Tree of Life
Or me.

Apple Trees

Apple trees so sweet—
What a treat!
Nature's gift to us.
Trees provide for all,
Be we rich, poor, saint, or fallen.

She gives freely.
Rainbow colors in her blossoms,
Sweet fragrance infuses
Her fruits and medicinal blends.

She breathes in carbon dioxide as we breathe it out.
She breathes out oxygen as we breathe it in.
Again, we win!

We sit in her shade as she cools our day.
As we lean against her trunk, she supports us so well.
If we listen to her, she has amazing stories to tell.
"Be like me," says the apple tree.

The Nature of Water

Water flowing wants to be in motion,
One drop forever seeking its ocean.

Life abounds all around.
Can you truly hear water's amazing sounds?

Drops gather as friends are traveling together,
For that is their true nature.

If water is captured and contained,
The life of water is but in vain.
It stagnates and changes its structure;
What once was clear
Is smeared.

It cries to go with the flow
And be what it naturally is—
Free!
Free to find its ocean with
Rhythmic motion.

All earth's creatures and cosmic substances too
Flow with the river of life.
Together they attain whatever is their aim.
So much to gain!

We too can flow with the river of life,
Strife-free,
Or we can choose to stagnate, like water contained,
In vain,
Or worse yet grapple against the current,
So errant!

So join me, my friends:
May we stream along
With the river's song,
Attaining our goals and
Merging in the divine ocean
Where we belong.

Reflections

Reflections in a pool of water,
Mirror images behold:
What is it I see?
Is that me?

Reflections in the trees,
Fragrant blossoms I breathe:
Streams of sweetness fill me with glee.
What is it I see?
Is that me?

Reflections on the bees
As they buzz through their day,
Collecting pollen and making nectar along their way:
One lights on my arm and looks up at me.
What is it I see?
Is that me?

Reflections in my mind,
All emotions I observe:
When I look at you and you look at me,
What is it I see?
Is that me?

Forgotten Memory

Horns and hooves draw inward forces which feed the animal body,
Outward communication not allowed.
Time to nurture within,
Silently and peacefully.

Antlers radiate outward communication with all that is about.
Excitement, movement, reactions to senses—
So much revealed in an animal's eyes.

The Wise Ones say we have gone astray.
We have forgotten our essential nature.
What results is our own demise
Because we remember not
The words of the Wise.

I turned to Mother Nature for direction.
I need a resurrection!
Must clear my complexion.

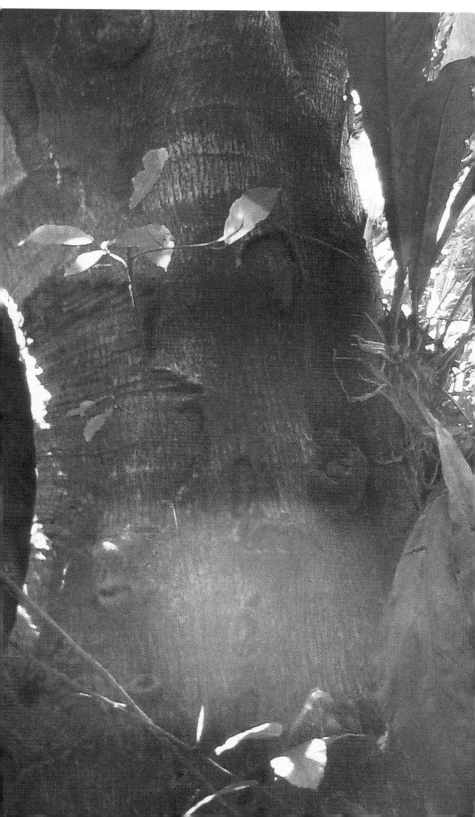

On Rollins Pond

The messages,
The wisdom within the trees,
Sing out to me.

"No rush.
Just be like me,"
Whispered the tree.

"See how I bend with the wind, rain, sleet, and snow,
Yet rooted deep, so as to keep my stand
As I grow.

"I breathe into you;
You breathe into me.
I am grateful to you;
You are grateful to me.
Together we be, we be, we be.

"When you hug me," announced the tree,
"You give me great joy.
You have noticed that I am here to help you grow.
Know you can love and be free like me,
An amazing tree!"

Back to the Forest

We pitch our tent in a small clearing,
Pines surrounding us.
I feel safe and loved in their presence.

Dark nights awaken with nature sounds.
Creatures abound;
In their pleasure, they reside together
Generation after generation,
Leaving seeds that root.
The chaos of the seed is a cosmos unto itself.

We in our camp, usually damp,
Listen.
Listen.
Listen.
"Human child," the forest declares,
"Nature is purposefully here
To teach you to forebear.

"Quiet your mind, humankind.
You are no longer blind.
Find you in me, me in you:
We.

Kayaking

Kayaking on a clear vast lake,
Forest all around,
Spirit energy abounds.
Pervasive in the silence of kayaking on this sparkling water
Was an invisible profound presence.

Food for the Senses

Sing with the birds.
Be open as a fragrant rose.
Let summer breezes flow as they may through your hair.
Taste the most succulent fruits that trees have to bear.
Hear the whispered messages of the willows.

Such is a formula for joyful living,
Something that keeps us believing
Goodness is a natural expression.

Seasons

It is written in the silver lining of the clouds.
It is written in the knots of the trees.
It is written especially in the brilliantly colored falling leaves.

It is spoken in the silence of the long winter nights:
Our spirits rise to greater heights.

Spring comes along with nature's melodious songs
Emanating all around.
Fragrances bursting forth with sweetness
Fill the soul with completeness.

The fire of summer's heat purifies body and mind.
We relax in our hammocks all day long.

The cycle is now complete.
Time to *om*,
Drift home.

Venus

Venus is the brightest planet
I see in the sky tonight,
Dispelling darkness with her love light.
What a magnificent sight!

She shines for all of us—
Can you not see?
Just gaze deeply in her eyes
And a message you'll receive.

She declares that we too are Venuses,
Yes!
We reflect her brilliant light.
Awake, O jewels of love light,
And shine in the darkest night.

Hold the lamp as Venus does,
A great gift you will bestow.
Dispel the darkness with your own love, bright
On planet Earth tonight!

Relationships:
out of tragedy came the strength
to understand how this all came to be.
I next turned what I learned into opportunity.

Everyday Love

Love,
Love,
Everywhere—
If you blink, it's here; blink again, it's there.

Such a packed commuter train
No place availed itself,
When a young father with his two small daughters appeared.
They entered that train;
Cannot explain, but
We all readjusted.
Behold!
Father and two small daughters
Seats together were bestowed.

Love,
Love,
Everywhere—
If you blink, it's here; blink again, it's there.

Butterfly Gardens

While awaiting our turn to purchase a ticket,
We glanced for a moment at a bright light spirit.
All but two years old,
She was dressed in frills of pink, purple, and gold.
Her eyes were closed; she smiled dreamily
While dancing to sweet music,
That charmed butterfly spirit.

We shed our sixty years as we entered her young sphere.
She spread her arms as wide as butterfly wings
And entered the garden twirling, swaying, dancing, and singing.
This tiny girl dressed in frills of pink, purple, and gold
Made our sixty years seem not so old.

Women

Women united in reclaiming their truth
Clear and cleanse from stories so old and buried
Anger and unworthiness that cause disease.
Uproot to open a portal for rejuvenation,
Transformation.

A shift in thinking
Brings a shift in action.
How mighty is this revolution!

Clarity

It takes clarity and confidence
To say no when everyone else is saying yes.

It takes clarity, confidence, and compassion
Not to engage in someone else's emotional reaction.

It takes clarity, confidence, compassion, and grace
To choose the moment that feels right for you
When others are angry with you for not
Choosing their own right moment.

It takes clarity, confidence, compassion, grace, and patience
When friends abandon you.

It takes clarity, confidence, compassion, grace, patience, and love
To set boundaries to loose yourself from
Life's demands.

It takes clarity, confidence, compassion, grace, patience, love, and
    detachment
To release your expectations of desired outcomes.

It takes wisdom
To live in the moment
And be,
Let be.

Gather

Gather together, we women,
That we may awaken
As one in this rebirth—
Renewal!
Let us sing who we are.
Let us nurture who we are.
Let us love who we are.
Let us express who we are.
Let us uplift all around
By the power of who we are.

Letting Go

No longer swept away by life's
Rush
Rush
Rush.

My life has become one that is more
Hush
Hush
Hush.

Let go of expectations, choosing
Exploration
Vacation
Illumination.

Real living,
Thanksgiving.

No Need

No need to think.
No need to speak.
No need to act.
No need at all.

Quiet mind
Says nothing at all.
It rests in the void,
Emerging in the soul.

Actions

Some actions
Are just
Not OK!

Pot of Gold

All that was taken away
Was not mine anyway,

Like a sweet melody
That came to my ear
Then left for someone else to hear.

And the letting go of pain—
Yes, that too—
Was not mine anyway.

The sword that pierced
Left me an opening
To invite a great awakening.

All I need to do is be who I am.
Time and truth will reveal my innocence.

It is not what others think.
It is not what I think.
It is what my intention is
That determines my gain.

Continue I must to live and love.
A moment will come
When I will receive
The pot of gold from above.

Thoughts

If it is true that my thoughts create my reality,
Then surely it will behoove me
To imagine only a sphere around me that is a
Loving,
Colorful
Horn of plenty.

May there be celestial songs sung
Accompanied by divine orchestras.
May they resound and
Create joyful smiles.

May kindness, sharing, and
Caring prevail,
A new world of peaceful living with
Playful interaction.

May everyone's needs be met
In both an earthly and a spiritual way,
Such that everyone will declare,
"What a fabulous day!"

Unconditional

I met a sweet Mexican man yesterday,
So gentle and kind,
Who saw a family in need.

With a wide-open smile,
He opened his wallet
And offered some pesos to a little girl.

With a shy grin, she stretched out her hand
To receive this gift from
This unassuming, generous man.

He continued his work,
Contented with himself,
As though no great deed were done.

A fleeting moment appeared to witness
The kindness of this sweet, gentle Mexican man.

Reminder

My spirit by its nature is joyful,
My thoughts by their nature are peaceful,
My expression by its nature is loving.
All these I dwell in.

When I see those I love in turmoil,
When I feel the pain they endure,
I at first enter their realm and then
Stop,
Step back,
Remind myself that my spirit by its nature is joyful.
My thoughts by their nature are peaceful.
My expression by its nature is loving.
All these I send to them.

As I sit here witnessing the creation from human minds,
As I sit here witnessing these polar opposites
     creation-destruction
     love-hate
     health-sickness
     joy-sorrow
I stop,
Step back,
Remind myself that my spirit by its nature is joyful.
My thoughts by their nature are peaceful.
My expression by its nature is loving.
All these I dwell in.

Why?

Why is it that I see the sun through the rain clouds?
Black swirls part to reveal rainbows.

Why is it that I see the brightness of the day?
The darkest of nights suddenly illuminates.

Why is it that all is just as it should be?
Chaos all around shifts us into new realms.

Stars and planets aglow
Let me know all I need to grow.
Trust the purpose
Without always understanding.

The complete picture is vast.
It is formed from darkness and light
To give us insight.

Walk

We go for a walk
Together or
Alone.
Destiny is the same:
Home.

Message from Divine Mother:
the only reason for our human existence is
to know our own divinity.

Do You Feel It?

Do you feel it?
Light is striking the planet.
They say it is a solar flare.
I say it is penetrating my soul,
Lifting me high,
Making my body light,
So it can merge with the One.

Do you feel it?
I see things—happenings—
A knowing that there is a purpose for all experiences.
I need not suppose or guess anymore.
Understanding has set in for all cause and effect,
Which is changing our DNA.
We will emerge new,
No more struggling or suffering.

Do you feel it?
All of a sudden, there is time to pause,
Notice divine plan revealed.
Mysteries unlock.

The search has ended for what I am seeking.
What I was striving for is right here
Inside me.
I found it because I paused one day,
And in that pause
The answer came.

Do you feel it?
When the answer arrived,
I bowed to it.
It consumed me.
No more fear—
Utter peace is here.

Extension of Life

It was not a dream;
The experience was real.
It lifted up my heart:
This to all I must reveal.

The night was as ordinary as most nights are.
I was soundly sleeping when appeared from afar
A warm glow.
A gentle alluring light force magnetically raised me
Out the night above my mortal self.

I knew it was He calling for me.
Somehow the timing was wrong.
It just could not be.

"Please, may I have more time?
There is so much … so much more to be done.
My love needs me, this I know.
Please let us continue to together grow."

He gently placed me back into myself.
This second chance was worth more than all the world's wealth.

He is allowing me more time to find my way,
To complete my life's work
For that final day.

From that evening on, I've feared not what lies beyond,
For in His love there is an immortal bond.
When it is my time to meet Him again,
I will open my arms and heart
And go with Him.

Sunshine

As long as You love me,
As long as You care,
Sunshine will be spread
Everywhere.

Silence

What is silence?
Where might it be?
It certainly is not here in the city!

Or is it?

Is silence on a mountaintop?
Well, let's see …
Nature truly chatters much in the forest.
Hmm … no silence here!

Or is it?

Maybe if I just sit,
I will find this elusive thing.
Oh, no! Thoughts are too many in this mind.
Cannot find silence, not here.

Or is it?

I let go of my hold,
Not a thought to enfold.
No noise around disturbs
My newfound soundless sound.

Silent Retreat

This little book is open;
Pen is in hand.
There is finally a free moment to
Write thoughts so grand.

This silent retreat has
Silenced my mind.
There is not even
A minuscule word to find!

Remember

Remember
All the little flowers
That blossom with the
Wonder of God's love.

We are those sweet flowers,
Budding,
Radiating,
Fragrantly
Divine.

Grace

Today I asked for the grace
To move forward.
Don't know what form it will take.

A message came to me:
All I need to do
Is let things effortlessly come.

It is not a message for me to
Reach out and cling,
For Grace has much of itself to bring.

May it show up at my doorstep.
May I recognize it as such.
May I embrace it and welcome it to
Renew every cell,
So I can tell
That within me
It will eternally dwell.

Service and duty:
Even the tiniest selfless service, however unnoticed by man,
is acknowledged by the Universe.

Nature Teacher

Perhaps it is the time to get in touch with Nature Teacher.
Oh, there comes and goes the tiniest swirly creature!
A gnat! Oops! Another one, just being who it is.

The gnat returns.
Closer to my face it pauses and
Looks deeply into my eyes as it passes by.

A small stream flows in the meadow near me.
As the water runs by, the drops seem to say,
"We will show you how to flow."
Then they trickle away.

"Breathe me in," whispers the breeze,
"Then rise up beaming!"

For a moment in time,
We connect to beget a glimpse of ourselves.
In the form of another we discover
The truth uncovered.

Forms of Love

All trees, so many varieties,
Love in tree form.

All birds, with their distinct songs,
Love in bird form.

All flowers, colorful and fragrant,
Love in flower form.

All creatures, microscopic and gigantic,
Love in creature form.

All people, each a beam of light in costume,
Love in human form.

All creation, one with the Great Spirit,
Love in creation form.

The Traveling Instrument

Piano, piano,
You have served so well,
Moved from there to here
And back to there again!
Tuned and voiced over and over,
Then …

Once prepared for a most
Melodious moment,
Ready, so ready for precious expression
As the pianist takes her seat …

All who listen,
All who deeply hear,
Discover a message in the song.

As the pianist and instrument merge in union Divine,
The audience is nourished with vibrations so fine!

Gratitude, applause, and cheers resound
By all who partake your richness.

Concert hall is now quiet.
Alone you await in your crate
So you can meet your fate:
Moved from here to there,
To be tuned and voiced all over again!

Earth Mother

Earth Mother cried out to me:

I give you all that you need.

I bestow splendid fruits and grains,
Quench your thirst with purest rains,
Entertain you at sunrise with brilliance, and
Soothe your eyes with the setting sun.

All God's glory will be showered on you,
You need only delight in me.

Bathe yourself in my healing waters.
Warm yourself in my sun's rays.
Love Me.
Care for me.
Cherish me,
Your Mother Earth.

Prayer for the Senses

Let me see others as loving spirits.
Let me be silent enough to listen.
Let me speak what is truth.
Let me breathe peacefully in and out.
Let me touch another's heart with helping hands.

No violence could ever withstand the
Harmony each day commands.

Patience

Life-changing shifts sometimes happen subtly:
We may expect them to be radical and full of forceful impact,
And sometimes they are.
The subtle ones, going on each ordinary day in ordinary ways,
Are the ones we notice if we have insight and patience.

Today

Today influences the next today.
An open window
Brings in refreshing air,
Rejuvenation, so that
The new today will uplift the next new today.

Open hearts are open windows which
Bring all beings together today.
They sing and dance merrily forth into the next new today.

Meeting Thich Nhat Hanh at Blue Cliff Monastery

The moment this tiny man appeared,
All harbored emotions cleared.
Tears and more tears and more tears,
Years and years of concealed fears,
Washed away by these streams.

How could this tiny man unknown to me
By his silent presence be the
Trigger that uprooted injury and pain
Which now became as it must—
Dust?

He said of ancestors, "They want to help."
All we need do is ask,
For they now see clearly and
Respond more dearly
To our heartfelt requests.

Breathe in,
Breathe out;
Center is within,
Not without.

Calm mind,
Calm body;
Peace within,
Peace without.

We are the cause of our own suffering.
Misperceptions and
Thoughts sent out come back to us,
An echoing.

Ode to Aunt Jeannie

Looking at your life, Aunt Jeannie, I recognize it as one of
  unconditional love.
You are a "mother" who did not give birth to her own son, but
Raised a nephew as her own.
Your generosity to all has been remarkable.
Your unfailing support to family and friends will be remembered
  forever.
Your life has been one of sacrifice, disappointments, courage, and
  forgiveness.
Your advice to all will be remembered and hopefully lived.

As you enter your ninth decade on this planet, you can certainly say,
"I gave my all to everyone."
All have benefitted; some acknowledge it, others do not.
Your messages are repeated at our every visit:
"Live simply so you can travel and experience how others live."
"Do everything in moderation."
"Do not ever stop working; it keeps your mind alive!"
"You might not be able to fix other people's problems, but you can
  always
Listen to them, and feed them soup and *salada*!"

You gave a home to your nephew,
You gave a home to his son.
You give encouragement to all of us in hard times.

Sometimes we listen.
Sometimes we do not.
We adjust our lives when we finally understand your wisdom.

All you have bestowed will be returned to you one day.
Your wings have sprouted.
You are ready to fly.
You are perched on a mountaintop looking over the land,
Ready to meet your Creator.
There is none greater!

Afterword

I have spent the past forty-four years as a traveling teacher, visiting homes and home schools both in the United States and abroad. During these years, I have developed an abounding respect for various cultures and the environments in which they thrive.

Experiencing the profound love that is expressed by both the wealthy and the impoverished for their families, and having witnessed the love that nature's creatures have for their young, I am able sometimes to see the elusive thread that connects us all. I am discovering that only a balanced human mind filled with gratitude and honor for the oneness of all creation can ultimately restore the health and prosperity of this planet Earth. I pray that our human family will choose to live with the human values that are innate in all, so that future generations will thrive and Mother Earth will stay alive.

Acknowledgments

It is with heartfelt appreciation that I thank my partner, Sergei Ivanov; my son, Phil Kanakis; and his partner, Holly Fischer, for all their patience, encouragement, and technical support. Without their loving interventions, this book would still be unpublished.

Several spiritual teachers and masters have blessed me with their teachings. I humbly thank my first teacher, Franciscan Friar Reverend Tom Costa, who supported me in my spiritual quest and sent me to India to meet Sathya Sai Baba, whose message is, simply, to serve society with love and humility, without exception. Through this we will know our divinity. He taught me self-confidence by assigning me tasks that seemed impossible to do. Only by God's grace did I successfully complete them.

Other great saints crossed my path, showering their blessings. I give my deepest gratitude to His Holiness the Dalai Lama (Tenzin Gyatso), whom I met in Daramsala, India, Amma Sri Karunamayi, Mata Amritanandamayi Devi, Mother Meera, and Thich Nhat Hanh. If I learned anything at all from these masters, it is that all forms of God are in alignment and all religions teach love, brotherhood of man, and the oneness of all sentient beings, which are sparks of Divinity.

About the Author

Christine Kanakis is a lifelong resident of the Hudson Valley, New York. She enjoys writing, gardening, long-distance swimming, hiking, and traveling both within the United States and abroad. She has explored nature in the Shawangunk, Catskill, and Adirondack mountains, and has studied nature with other biologists at the volcanoes and the inlet waters of Costa Rica. She has also explored Mexico's cenotes and learned about medicinal plants in the Sian Kan forest.

Christine's many trips to India have connected her with Universal Spirit as she studied under great spiritual masters.

Christine holds BS and MS degrees in education and science, and teaches math and science to private students and at home schools in the US and overseas. Influenced by her agricultural studies with Shumei farmers (Japanese agriculturalists) in the Catskill Mountains and by Rudolf Steiner's biodynamic farming degree program at Chestnut Ridge, New York, Christine includes all she has learned about nature and nutrition in her teaching and writing.

Printed in the United States
by Baker & Taylor Publisher Services